Stories from the Old Testament © Frances Lincoln Limited 1996

First published in Great Britain in 1996 by Frances Lincoln Limited,
4 Torriano Mews, Torriano Avenue, London NW5 2RZ

British Library Cataloguing in Publication Data available on request.

ISBN 0-7112-1084-5

Set in Bembo and Poetica Chancery IV

Printed in Hong Kong
1 3 5 7 9 8 6 4 2

STORIES FROM
THE OLD TESTAMENT

FRANCES LINCOLN

CONTENTS

THE CREATION

IN THE BEGINNING God created the heaven and the earth. And the earth was without form, and void; and darkness was upon the face of the deep. And the Spirit of God moved upon the face of the waters.

And God said, "Let there be light": and there was light. And God saw the light, that it was good: and God divided the light from the darkness. And God called the light Day, and the darkness Night. And the evening and the morning were the first day.

And God said, "Let there be a firmament in the midst of the waters, and let it divide the waters from the waters": and it was so. And God called the firmament Heaven. And the evening and the morning were the second day.

And God said, "Let the waters under the heaven be gathered together unto one place, and let the dry land appear": and it was so. And God called the dry land Earth; and the gathering together of the waters called he Seas: and God saw that it was good. And God said, "Let the earth bring forth grass, the herb yielding seed and the fruit tree yielding fruit after his kind, whose seed is in itself, upon the earth": and it was so. And the evening and the morning were the third day.

And God said, "Let there be lights in the firmament of heaven to divide the day from the night; and let them be for signs, and for seasons, and for days and years": And God made two great lights; the greater light to rule the day, and the lesser light to rule the night: he made the stars also. And God set them in the firmament of heaven to give light upon the earth. And the evening and the morning were the fourth day.

And God said, "Let the waters bring forth abundantly the moving creature that hath life, and fowl that may fly above the earth." And God created great whales, and every living creature which the waters brought forth, and every winged fowl after his kind: and God saw that it was good. And God blessed them, saying, "Be fruitful, and multiply." And the evening and the morning were the fifth day.

And God said, "Let the earth bring forth the living creature after his kind, cattle, and creeping thing, and beast of the earth after his kind": and it was so.

And God said, "Let us make man in our image, after our likeness: and let them have dominion over the fish of the sea, and over the fowl of the air, and over the cattle, and over all the earth."

So God created man in his own image, in the image of God created he him; male and female, created he them. And God blessed them, and God said unto them, "Be fruitful, and multiply, and replenish the earth, and subdue it." And God saw every thing that he had made, and behold, it was very good. And the evening and the morning were the sixth day.

And God blessed the seventh day, and sanctified it: because in it he had rested from all his work.

THE GARDEN OF EDEN

AND THE LORD GOD formed man of the dust of the ground, and breathed into his nostrils the breath of life; and man became a living soul.

And the Lord God planted a garden eastward in Eden; and there he put the man whom he had formed. And out of the ground made the Lord God to grow every tree that is pleasant to the sight, and good for food; the tree of life also grew in the midst of the garden, and the tree of knowledge of good and evil. And a river went out of Eden to water the garden.

And the Lord God took the man, and put him into the garden of Eden to dress it and to keep it.

And the Lord God commanded the man, saying, "Of every tree of the garden thou mayst freely eat: but of the tree of the knowledge of good and evil, thou shalt not eat of it: for in the day that thou eatest thereof, thou shalt surely die."

And the Lord God said, "It is not good that the man should be alone; I will make him an help meet for him."

And out of the ground the Lord God formed every beast of the field, and every fowl of the air; and brought them unto Adam to see what he would call them: and whatsoever Adam called every living creature, that was the name thereof.

And Adam gave names to all cattle, and to the fowl of the air, and to every beast of the field; but for Adam there was not found an help meet for him.

And the Lord God caused a deep sleep to fall upon Adam, and he slept; and he took one of his ribs, and closed up the flesh instead thereof; and the rib, which the Lord God had taken from the man, made he a woman, and brought her unto the man.

And Adam said, "This is now bone of my bones, and flesh of my flesh; she shall be called Woman, because she was taken out of Man."

Therefore shall a man leave his father and his mother, and shall cleave unto his wife: and they shall be one flesh.

And they were both naked, the man and his wife, and were not ashamed.

THE FALL OF ADAM AND EVE

NOW THE SERPENT WAS more subtil than any beast of the field. And he said unto the woman, "Hath God said, 'Ye shall not eat of every tree of the garden?'"

And the woman said unto the serpent, "Of the fruit of the tree which is in the midst of the garden, God hath said, 'Ye shall not eat of it, neither shall ye touch it, lest ye die.'"

And the serpent said unto the woman, "Ye shall not surely die: for God doth know that in the day ye eat thereof, then your eyes shall be opened, and ye shall be as gods, knowing good and evil."

And when the woman saw that the tree was good for food, and a tree to be desired to make one wise, she took of the fruit thereof, and did eat, and gave also unto her husband; and he did eat. And the eyes of them both were opened, and they knew that they were naked; and they sewed fig leaves together, and made themselves aprons.

And they heard the voice of the Lord God walking in the garden in the cool of the day; and Adam and his wife hid themselves from the presence of the Lord God amongst the trees of the garden.

And the Lord God called unto Adam and said unto him, "Where art thou?" And he said, "I heard thy voice in the garden, and I was afraid, because I was naked; and I hid myself."

And he said, "Who told thee thou wast naked? Hast thou eaten of the tree whereof I commanded thee that thou shouldest not eat?"

And the man said, "The woman whom thou gavest to be with me, she gave me of the tree, and I did eat."

And the Lord God said unto the woman, "What is this that thou hast done?" And the woman said, "The serpent beguiled me, and I did eat."

And the Lord God said unto the serpent, "Because thou hast done this, thou art cursed above all cattle, and above every beast of the field; upon thy belly shalt thou go, and dust shalt thou eat all the days of thy life. And I will put enmity between thee and the woman, and between her seed and thy seed; it shall bruise thy head, and thou shalt bruise his heel."

Unto the woman he said, "I will greatly multiply thy sorrow and thy conception; in sorrow thou shalt bring forth children; and thy desire shall be to thy husband, and he shall rule over thee."

And unto Adam he said, "Cursed is the ground for thy sake; in sorrow shalt thou eat of it all the days of thy life. In the sweat of thy face shalt thou eat bread till thou return unto the ground; for dust thou art and unto dust shalt thou return." So he drove out the man; and he placed at the east of the garden of Eden Cherubims, and a flaming sword which turned every way, to keep the way of the tree of life.

❖ GENESIS 3 ❖

NOAH'S ARK

Grieved by men's wickedness, God sends a flood to destroy all life on earth.
Noah is righteous, so God warns him, and gives him special instructions.

AND GOD said unto Noah, "Make thee an ark of gopher wood; rooms shalt thou make in the ark, and shalt pitch it within and without with pitch. A window shalt thou make to the ark; and the door of the ark shalt thou set in the side thereof; with lower, second, and third stories shalt thou make it.

And, behold, I, even I, do bring a flood of waters upon the earth, to destroy all flesh wherein is the breath of life, from under heaven; and everything that is in the earth shall die. But with thee will I establish my covenant; and thou shalt come into the ark, thou, and thy sons, and thy wife, and thy sons' wives with thee. And of every living thing of all flesh, two of every sort shalt thou bring into the ark, to keep them alive with thee; they shall be male and female. And take thou unto thee of all food that is eaten, and thou shalt gather it to thee; and it shall be for food for thee, and for them."

Thus did Noah; according to all that God commanded him, so did he.

And the Lord said unto Noah, "Come thou and all thy house into the ark; for thee have I seen righteous before me in this generation. For yet seven days, and I will cause it to rain upon the earth forty days and forty nights; and every living substance that I have made will I destroy from off the face of the earth."

And Noah went in, and his sons, and his wife, and his sons' wives with him, into the ark, because of the waters of the flood. Of clean beasts, and of beasts that are not clean, and of fowls, and of everything that creepeth upon the earth, there went in two and two unto Noah into the ark, the male and the female, as God commanded Noah.

And it came to pass after seven days, that the waters of the flood were upon the earth; the same day were all the fountains of the great deep broken up, and the windows of heaven were opened. And the rain was upon the earth forty days and forty nights.

And the waters prevailed exceedingly upon the earth. Fifteen cubits upwards did the waters prevail; and the mountains were covered.

And all flesh died that moved upon the earth, both of fowl, and of cattle, and of beast, and of every creeping thing that creepeth upon the face of the earth, and every man: and Noah only remained alive, and they that were with him in the ark.

❖ GENESIS 6 & 7 ❖

AFTER THE FLOOD

After forty days, the rain stops, and eventually the flood begins to subside.
The ark comes to rest on the tip of Mount Ararat.

AND IT CAME to pass that Noah opened the window of the ark which he had made: and he sent forth a raven, which went forth to and fro until the waters were dried up from off the earth. Also he sent forth a dove from him, to see if the waters were abated; but the dove found no rest for the sole of her foot, and she returned unto him into the ark, for the waters were on the face of the whole earth.

And he stayed yet another seven days; and again he sent forth the dove; and the dove came in to him in the evening; and, lo, in her mouth was an olive leaf pluckt off: so Noah knew that the waters were abated from off the earth.

And he stayed yet another seven days; and sent forth the dove; which returned not again unto him any more. And it came to pass that Noah removed the covering of the ark, and looked, and, behold, the face of the ground was dry.

And God spake unto Noah, saying, "Go forth of the ark, thou, and thy wife, and thy sons, and thy sons' wives with thee. Bring forth every living thing that is with thee, that they may breed, and be fruitful, and multiply upon the earth."

And Noah went forth, and builded an altar unto the Lord; and took of every clean beast, and of every clean fowl, and offered burnt offerings upon the altar.

And the Lord smelled a sweet savour; and the Lord said in his heart, "I will not again curse the ground for man's sake; for the imagination of man's heart is evil from his youth; neither will I again smite every living thing. While the earth remaineth, seedtime and harvest, and cold and heat, and summer and winter, and day and night shall not cease."

And God spake unto Noah, saying, "And, behold, I do set my bow in the cloud, and it shall be for a token of a covenant between me and the earth. And it shall come to pass, when I bring a cloud over the earth, that the bow shall be seen in the cloud; and I will remember my covenant, which is between me and you and every living creature; and the waters shall no more become a flood to destroy all flesh. This is the token of the covenant, which I have established between me and all flesh that is upon the earth."

And Noah lived after the flood three hundred and fifty years. And all the days of Noah were nine hundred and fifty years: and he died.

THE TOWER OF BABEL

*In the centuries after the flood, Noah's descendants gradually spread out over
the face of the earth. Because they all come from the same family,
they speak a common language, and understand each other perfectly.*

AND THE WHOLE earth was of one language, and of one speech.

And it came to pass, as they journeyed from the east, that they found a plain in the land of Shinar; and they dwelt there.

And they said one to another, "Go to, let us make bricks, and burn them thoroughly." And they had brick for stone, and slime had they for morter.

And they said, "Go to, let us build a city and a tower, whose top may reach unto heaven; and let us make us a name, lest we be scattered abroad upon the face of the whole earth."

And the Lord came down to see the city and the tower, which the children of men builded.

And the Lord said, "Behold, the people is one, and they have all one language; and this they begin to do: and now nothing will be restrained from them, which they have imagined to do.

Go to, let us go down, and there confound their language, that they may not understand one another's speech."

So the Lord scattered them abroad from thence upon the face of all the earth: and they left off to build the city.

Therefore is the name of it called Babel; because the Lord did there confound the language of all the earth; and from thence did the Lord scatter them abroad upon the face of all the earth.

ABRAHAM AND ISAAC

God promises Abraham, one of Noah's descendants, that in their old age he and his wife will have a son, who will grow up to be the founder of a great nation. When Isaac is born, his parents rejoice - but later God gives Abraham a terrible test of faith.

AND GOD DID tempt Abraham, and said unto him, "Take now thy son, thine only son Isaac, whom thou lovest, and get thee into the land of Moriah; and offer him there for a burnt offering upon one of the mountains which I will tell thee of."

And Abraham rose up early in the morning, and saddled his ass, and took two of his young men with him, and Isaac his son, and clave the wood for the burnt offering, and went unto the place of which God had told him. Then on the third day Abraham lifted up his eyes, and saw the place afar off.

And Abraham said unto his young men, "Abide ye here with the ass; and I and the lad will go yonder and worship, and come again to you."

And Abraham took the wood of the burnt offering, and laid it upon Isaac his son; and he took the fire in his hand, and a knife; and they went both of them together.

And Isaac spake unto Abraham his father, and said, "My father, behold the fire and the wood: but where is the lamb for a burnt offering?"

And Abraham said, "My son, God will provide himself a lamb for a burnt offering": so they went both of them together.

And they came to the place which God had told him of; and Abraham built an altar there, and laid the wood in order, and bound Isaac his son, and laid him on the altar upon the wood. And Abraham stretched forth his hand, and took the knife to slay his son.

And the angel of the Lord called unto him out of heaven, and said, "Abraham, Abraham: lay not thy hand upon the lad, neither do thou any thing unto him: for now I know that thou fearest God, seeing thou hast not witheld thy son, thine only son from me."

And Abraham lifted up his eyes, and looked, and beheld behind him a ram caught in a thicket by his horns: and Abraham went and took the ram, and offered him up for a burnt offering in the stead of his son.

And the angel of the Lord called unto Abraham out of heaven a second time, and said, "By myself have I sworn, saith the Lord, because thou hast done this thing, and has not witheld thy son, thine only son: that in blessing I will bless thee, and in multiplying I will multiply thy seed as the stars in heaven, and as the sand which is upon the sea shore: and in thy seed shall all the nations of the earth be blessed; because thou hast obeyed my voice."

REBEKAH AT THE WELL

*Abraham does not want Isaac to marry a Canaanite woman. He sends his servant Eliezer to fetch
Isaac a wife from their homeland - but how is Eliezer to find the right bride?*

AND THE SERVANT took ten camels of the camels of his master: and he arose, and went to Mesopotamia, unto the city of Nahor.

And he made his camels to kneel down without the city by a well of water at the time of the evening, even the time that women go out to draw water.

And he said, "O Lord God of my master Abraham, I pray thee, send me good speed this day, and shew kindness unto my master. Behold, I stand here by the well; and the daughters of the men of the city come out to draw water: let it come to pass that the damsel to whom I shall say, 'Let down thy pitcher, I pray thee, that I may drink,' and she shall say, 'Drink, and I will give thy camels drink also,' let the same be she that thou hast appointed for thy servant Isaac." And it came to pass before he had done speaking that, behold, Rebekah came out, with her pitcher upon her shoulder.

And the damsel was very fair to look upon, a virgin, neither had any man known her; and she went down to the well, and filled her pitcher, and came up. And the servant ran to meet her, and said, "Let me, I pray thee, drink a little water of thy pitcher."

And she said, "Drink, my lord," and she hasted and let down her pitcher upon her hand.

And when she had done giving him drink, she said, "I will draw water for thy camels also." And she hasted, and emptied her pitcher into the trough, and ran again unto the well to draw water, and drew for all his camels.

And it came to pass, as the camels had done drinking, that the man said, "Whose daughter art thou? Tell me, I pray thee."

And she said unto him, "I am the daughter of Bethuel the son of Milcah, which she bare unto Nahor." And the man bowed down his head, and said, "Blessed be the Lord God of my master Abraham: the Lord led me to the house of my master's brethren." And the damsel ran, and told them of her mother's house these things.

And the man came in to the house, *and told his errand.* And they called Rebekah, and said unto her, "Wilt thou go with this man?" And she said, "I will go." And the servant took Rebekah, and went his way.

And Isaac went out to meditate in the field at the eventide: and he lifted up his eyes, and saw, and behold, the camels were coming.

And Rebekah lifted up her eyes, and when she saw Isaac, she lighted off the camel. And Isaac brought her into his mother Sarah's tent, and took Rebekah, and she became his wife; and he loved her: and Isaac was comforted after his mother's death.

GENESIS 24

JOSEPH AND HIS BROTHERS

*Isaac's grandson Joseph is sold as a slave by his older brothers. Years later, when they travel to Egypt to buy food,
they do not realise that the mighty governor at whose feet they tremble is their own brother.
He recognises them, however …*

AND JOSEPH COMMANDED the steward of his house, saying, "Fill the men's sacks with food, as much as they can carry, and put my silver cup in the sack's mouth of the youngest." And he did according to the word that Joseph had spoken.

As soon as the morning was light, the men were sent away. And when they were gone out of the city, and not yet far off, Joseph said unto his steward, "Up, follow after them; and when thou dost overtake them, say, 'Wherefore have ye rewarded evil for good? Is not this the cup in which my lord drinketh? Ye have done evil in so doing.'" And the steward overtook them, and spake unto them the same words.

Then they speedily took down every man his sack to the ground; and opened every man his sack. And he searched, and began at the eldest and left at the youngest: and the cup was found in Benjamin's sack.

Then they rent their clothes, and laded every man his ass, and returned to the city. And Judah and his brethren came to Joseph's house, and fell before him on the ground. And Judah said, "What shall we say unto my lord? What shall we speak, or how shall we clear ourselves? Behold, we are my lord's servants, both we, and he also with whom the cup is found."

And Joseph said, "God forbid that I should do so: but the man in whose hand the cup is found, he shall be my servant; and as for you, get you up in peace unto your father."

Then Judah said, "O my lord, it shall come to pass, when our father seeth that the lad is not with us, that he will die: and thy servants will bring down his gray hairs with sorrow to the grave. Now therefore, I pray thee, let me abide instead of the lad a bondman to my lord; and let the lad go with his brethren."

Then Joseph wept aloud, and said unto his brethren, "I am Joseph, your brother, whom ye sold into Egypt. Haste ye, and go up to my father, and say unto him, Thus saith your son Joseph: God hath made me lord of all Egypt: come down to me and tarry not." And he kissed all his brethren, and wept upon them: and after that his brethren talked with him.

And they went up out of Egypt into the land of Canaan, unto Jacob their father, and told him, saying, "Joseph is yet alive, and he is governor over all the land of Egypt." And when they told him all the words of Joseph, the spirit of Jacob their father revived. And he said, "It is enough; Joseph my son is yet alive: I will go and see him before I die."

❖ GENESIS 44 & 45 ❖

MOSES IN THE BULRUSHES

After Joseph's death, the Israelites stay in Egypt.
Years pass, and soon their descendants fill the land.

NOW THERE AROSE up a new king over Egypt, which knew not Joseph. And he said unto his people, "Behold, the people of Israel are more and mightier than we. Come on, let us deal wisely with them; lest they multiply, and it come to pass that, when there falleth out any war, they join unto our enemies, and fight against us."

Therefore they did set over them taskmasters to afflict them with their burdens.

And they built for Pharaoh treasure cities, Pithom and Raamses. And the Egyptians made their lives bitter with hard bondage, in morter, and in brick, and in all manner of service in the field: all their service, wherein they made them serve, was with rigour.

And Pharaoh charged all his people saying, "Every *Hebrew* son that is born, ye shall cast into the river, and every daughter ye shall save alive."

And there went a man of the house of Levi, and took to wife a daughter of Levi. And the woman conceived, and bare a son: and when she saw him that he was a goodly child, she hid him three months.

And when she could no longer hide him, she took for him an ark of bulrushes, and daubed it with slime and with pitch, and put the child therein; and she laid it in the flags by the river's brink. And his sister stood afar off, to wit what would be done to him.

And the daughter of Pharaoh came down to wash herself at the river; and when she saw the ark among the flags, she sent her maid to fetch it. And when she had opened it, she saw the child: and behold, the babe wept. And she had compassion on him, and said, "This is one of the Hebrews' children."

Then said his sister to Pharaoh's daughter, "Shall I go and call to thee a nurse of the Hebrew women, that she may nurse the child for thee?"

And Pharaoh's daughter said to her, "Go." And the maid went and called the child's mother.

And Pharaoh's daughter said unto her, "Take this child away and nurse it for me, and I will give thee wages." And the woman took the child, and nursed it.

And the child grew, and she brought him unto Pharaoh's daughter, and he became her son. And she called his name Moses: and she said, "Because I drew him out of the water."

EXODUS 1 & 2

THE CROSSING OF THE RED SEA

Moses asks Pharaoh to let the Israelites leave Egypt. Pharaoh refuses, but when the Lord sends a plague that kills the oldest child in every Egyptian family, he gives in. Guided by a pillar of cloud by day and a pillar of fire by night, the Israelites set out.

AND THE HEART of Pharaoh and of his servants was turned against the people, and they said, "Why have we done this, that we have let Israel go from serving us?"

And he took six hundred chariots, and pursued after the children of Israel, and overtook them encamping by the sea. And when Pharaoh drew nigh, the children of Israel lifted up their eyes, and, behold, the Egyptians marched after them; and they were sore afraid.

And Moses said unto his people, "Fear ye not, stand still, and see the salvation of the Lord, which he will shew to you today: for the Egyptians whom ye have seen today, ye shall see them no more for ever. The Lord shall fight for you, and ye shall hold your peace."

And the angel of God, which went before the camp of Israel, removed and went behind them; and the pillar of cloud went from before their face, and stood behind them. And it came between the camp of the Egyptians and the camp of Israel; and it was a cloud and darkness to them, but it gave light to these: so that one came not near the other all the night.

And Moses stretched out his hand over the sea; and the Lord caused the sea to go back by a strong east wind all night, and made the sea dry land, and the waters were divided.

And the children of Israel went into the midst of the sea upon the dry ground: and the waters were a wall unto them on their right hand, and on their left. And the Egyptians pursued, and went in after them, all Pharaoh's horses, his chariots, and his horsemen.

And it came to pass that in the morning the Lord looked through the pillar of fire and of the cloud, and troubled the host of the Egyptians, and took off their chariot wheels, that they drove them heavily: so that the Egyptians said, "Let us flee from the face of Israel; for the Lord fighteth for them against the Egyptians."

And the Lord said unto Moses, "Stretch out thine hand over the sea, that the waters may come again upon the Egyptians, upon their chariots, and upon their horsemen."

And Moses stretched forth his hand over the sea. And the waters returned, and covered the chariots, and the horsemen, and all the host of Pharaoh that came into the sea after them; there remained not so much as one of them.

Thus the Lord saved Israel out of the hand of the Egyptians, and Israel saw the Egyptians dead upon the sea shore. And Israel saw that great work which the Lord did upon the Egyptians: and the people feared the Lord, and believed the Lord, and his servant Moses.

❖ EXODUS 14 ❖

THE TEN COMMANDMENTS

After the Lord leads the Israelites out of Egypt, he calls Moses up on to Mount Sinai.
Thunder crashes and the earth shakes as he gives Moses the laws for his chosen people to obey.

AND THE LORD CALLED Moses up to the top of the mount; and Moses went up. And God spake these words, saying:

"I am the Lord thy God, which have brought thee out of the land of Egypt, out of the house of bondage. Thou shalt have no other gods before me.

Thou shalt not make unto thee any graven image, or any likeness of any thing that is in heaven above, or that is in the earth beneath, or that is in the water under the earth. Thou shalt not bow down to them, nor serve them: for I the Lord thy God am a jealous God, visiting the iniquity of the fathers upon the children unto the third and fourth generation of them that hate me; and shewing mercy unto thousands of them that love me, and keep my commandments.

Thou shalt not take the name of the Lord thy God in vain; for the Lord will not hold him guiltless that taketh his name in vain.

Remember the sabbath day, to keep it holy. Six days shalt thou labour, and do all thy work: but the seventh day is the sabbath of the Lord thy God: in it thou shalt not do any work, thou, nor thy son, nor thy daughter, nor thy maidservant, nor thy cattle, nor thy stranger that is within thy gates. For in six days the Lord made heaven and earth, the sea, and all that in them is, and rested the seventh day: wherefore the Lord blessed the sabbath day, and hallowed it.

Honour thy father and thy mother, that thy days may be long upon the land which the Lord thy God giveth thee.

Thou shalt not kill.

Thou shalt not commit adultery.

Thou shalt not steal.

Thou shalt not bear false witness against thy neighbour.

Thou shalt not covet thy neighbour's house, thou shalt not covet thy neighbour's wife, nor his manservant, nor his maidservant, nor his ox, nor his ass, nor any thing that is thy neighbour's."

And all the people saw the thunderings, and the lightnings, and the noise of the trumpet, and the mountain smoking: and when the people saw it, they removed, and stood afar off. And they said unto Moses, "Speak thou with us, and we will hear: but let not God speak with us, lest we die."

And Moses said unto the people, "Fear not: for God is come to prove you, and that his fear may be before your faces, that ye sin not."

❖ EXODUS 19 & 20 ❖

RUTH AND NAOMI

Naomi is an Israelite. When her husband and sons die in distant Moab, she sets her heart on returning to Bethlehem.
Ruth, her Moabite daughter-in-law, refuses to leave her, even at the cost of becoming an exile herself.

SO NAOMI RETURNED, and Ruth, her daughter-in-law, with her: and they came to Bethlehem in the beginning of barley harvest.

And Naomi had a kinsman of her husband's, a mighty man of wealth; and his name was Boaz. And Ruth said unto Naomi, "Let me now go to the field, and glean ears of corn after him in whose sight I shall find grace." And she said unto her, "Go, my daughter."

And Ruth went, and came, and gleaned in the field after the reapers: and her hap was to light on a part of the field belonging unto Boaz. And, behold, Boaz came from Bethlehem, and said, "Whose damsel is this?" And his servant answered, "It is the damsel that came back with Naomi out of the country of Moab."

Then said Boaz unto Ruth, "Go not to glean in another field, neither go from hence, but abide here fast by my maidens. Let thine eyes be on the field that they do reap, and go thou after them: and when thou art athirst, go unto the vessels, and drink of that which the young men have drawn."

Then she fell on her face, and said unto him, "Why have I found grace in thine eyes, that thou shouldest take knowledge of me, seeing I am a stranger?"

And Boaz answered and said unto her, "It hath fully been shewed me, all that thou hast done unto thy mother-in-law since the death of thine husband: how thou hast left thy father and thy mother, and the land of thy nativity, and art come unto a people which thou knewest not heretofore. The Lord recompense thy work, and a full reward be given thee of the Lord God of Israel, under whose wings thou art come to trust."

Then she said, "Let me find favour in thy sight, my lord; for that thou hast comforted me, and for that thou hast spoken friendly unto thy handmaid, though I be not like unto one of thine handmaidens."

And when she was risen up to glean, Boaz commanded his young men, saying, "Let her glean even among the sheaves, and reproach her not." So she kept fast by the maidens of Boaz to glean unto the end of barley harvest and of wheat harvest . . .

And Boaz took Ruth, and she was his wife: and when he went in unto her, the Lord gave her conception, and she bare a son.

And the women said unto Naomi, "Blessed be the Lord, which hath not left thee this day without a kinsman. He shall be unto thee a restorer of thy life, and a nourisher of thine old age: for thy daughter-in-law, which loveth thee, which is better to thee than seven sons, hath born him."

And Naomi took the child, and laid it in her bosom.

DAVID AND GOLIATH

*The Philistines are at war with Israel. Their mighty champion, the giant Goliath, challenges the Israelites
to send a man against him in single combat. No one dares accept until, one day, Ruth's great-grandson,
a shepherd-boy called David, comes to visit his brothers in King Saul's army.*

AND, BEHOLD, THERE came up the champion, Goliath by name, out of the armies of the Philistines, and spake according to the same words. And all the men of Israel, when they saw the man, fled from him, and were sore afraid.

And David spake to the men that stood by him, saying, "Who is this uncircumcised Philistine, that he should defy the armies of the living God?" And when the words were heard which David spake, they rehearsed them before Saul: and he sent for him.

And David said to Saul, "Let no man's heart fail because of him; thy servant will go and fight with this Philistine."

And Saul said to David, "Thou art not able to go against this Philistine to fight with him: for thou art but a youth, and he a man of war from his youth."

And David said unto Saul, "Thy servant kept his father's sheep, and there came a lion, and a bear, and took a lamb out of the flock. And I went out after him, and smote him, and slew him. The Lord that delivered me out of the paw of the lion, and out of the paw of the bear, he will deliver me out of the hand of this Philistine." And Saul said unto David, "Go, and the Lord be with thee."

And David took his staff in his hand, and chose him five smooth stones out of the brook, and put them in a shepherd's bag which he had, even in a scrip; and his sling was in his hand; and he drew near to the Philistine.

And when the Philistine looked about, and saw David, he disdained him: for he was but a youth, and ruddy, and of a fair countenance. And the Philistine said to David, "Come to me, and I will give thy flesh unto the fowls of the air, and to the beasts of the field."

Then said David to the Philistine, "Thou comest to me with a sword, and with a spear, and with a shield: but I come to thee in the name of the Lord of hosts, the God of the armies of Israel, whom thou hast defied. This day will the Lord deliver thee into mine hand; and I will smite thee, and take thine head from thee; that all the earth may know that there is a God in Israel."

And David put his hand in his bag, and took thence a stone, and slang it, and smote the Philistine in the forehead; and he fell upon his face to the earth.

And David ran, and stood upon the Philistine, and took his sword, and cut off his head therewith. And when the Philistines saw their champion was dead, they fled.

❖ 1 SAMUEL 17 ❖

THE JUDGMENT OF SOLOMON

In a dream, King David's son Solomon asks the Lord for the wisdom to rule Israel wisely. The Lord grants his prayer, promising riches, honour and long life, if the king obeys the Lord's commands.

AND SOLOMON AWOKE; and behold, it was a dream. And he came to Jerusalem, and stood before the ark of the covenant of the Lord, and offered up burnt offerings, and peace offerings, and made a feast to all his servants.

Then came there two women unto the king, and stood before him.

And the one woman said, "O my lord, I and this woman dwell in one house; and I was delivered of a child with her in the house. And it came to pass the third day after that I was delivered, that this woman was delivered also; there was no stranger with us in the house, save we two. And this woman's child died in the night; because she overlaid it.

And she arose at midnight, and took my son from beside me, while thine handmaid slept, and laid it in her bosom, and laid her dead child in my bosom. And when I arose in the morning to give my child suck, behold, it was dead: but when I had considered it in the morning, behold, it was not my son, which I did bare."

And the other woman said, "No, but the dead is thy son, and the living is my son." Thus they spake before the king.

And the king said, "Bring me a sword." And they brought a sword before the king.

And the king said, "Divide the living child in two, and give half to one and half to the other."

Then spake the woman whose the living child was, "O my lord, give her the living child, and in no wise slay it." But the other said, "Let it be neither mine nor thine, but divide it."

Then the king answered and said, "Give her the living child, and in no wise slay it. She is the mother thereof."

And all Israel heard of the judgment which the king had judged; and they feared the king: for they saw that the wisdom of God was in him, to do judgment.

BELSHAZZAR'S FEAST

Long after King Solomon's death, Nebuchadnezzar, the king of Babylon, captures Jerusalem. At a great feast, his son
King Belshazzar serves wine in precious goblets which his father took from the Lord's temple. Suddenly a dreadful omen appears.

IN THE SAME HOUR came forth fingers of a man's hand, and wrote over against the candlestick upon the plaster of the wall of the king's palace.

Then the king's countenance was changed and his knees smote one against another. And the king spake and said to the wise men of Babylon, "Whosoever shall read this writing, and shew me the interpretation thereof, shall be clothed with scarlet, and have a chain of gold about his neck, and shall be the third ruler in the kingdom." Then came in all the king's wise men: but they could not read the writing.

Now the queen said, "O king, live for ever: let not thy thoughts trouble thee, nor let thy countenance be changed: there is a man in thy kingdom in whom is the spirit of the holy gods; now let Daniel be called, and he will shew the interpretation."

Then was Daniel brought in before the king. And the king said, "I have even heard of thee, that the spirit of the gods is in thee, and that light and understanding and excellent wisdom is found in thee. If thou canst read the writing, and make known to me the interpretation thereof, thou shalt be clothed with scarlet, and have a chain of gold about thy neck, and be the third ruler in the kingdom."

Then Daniel answered, "O thou king, the most high God gave Nebuchadnezzar thy father a kingdom, and majesty, and glory, and honour: and for the majesty that he gave him, all people, nations and languages, trembled and feared before him. But when his heart was lifted up, and his mind hardened in pride, he was deposed from his kingly throne, and they took his glory from him: and he was driven from the sons of men: and his heart was made like the beasts; they fed him with grass like oxen, and his body was wet with the dew of heaven; till he knew that the most high God rules in the kingdom of men, and that he appointeth over it whomsoever he will.

And thou his son, O Belshazzar, hast not humbled thine heart, though thou knewest all this; but has lifted up thyself against the Lord of heaven. Then was the part of the hand sent from him; and this writing was written. MENE; God has numbered thy kingdom, and finished it. TEKEL; Thou art weighed in the balance, and art found wanting. PERES; Thy kingdom is divided, and given to the Medes and Persians."

In that night was Belshazzar the king of the Chaldeans slain. And Darius the Median took his kingdom, being about threescore and two years old.

❖ DANIEL 5 ❖

King Darius appoints Daniel president over the kingdom of one hundred and twenty princes. Jealous of Daniel's growing power, the princes persuade Darius to sign a decree "according to the Medes and the Persians": for thirty days, no petitions may be made except to the king himself, on pain of being cast into the lions' den. Untroubled, Daniel continues to pray to God as before.

THEN THEY CAME near, and spake before the king: "Hast thou not signed a decree, that every man that shall ask a petition of any God or man within thirty days, save of thee, O king, shall be cast into the den of lions?" The king answered and said, "The thing is true, according to the law of the Medes and the Persians, which altereth not."

Then answered they and said, "Daniel regardeth not thee, O king, nor the decree that thou hast signed, but maketh his petition three times a day."

Then the king was sore displeased with himself, and he laboured till the going down of the sun to deliver Daniel. Then these men assembled unto the king and said unto the king, "Know, O king, that the law of the Medes and the Persians is, That no decree nor statute which the king establisheth may be changed."

Then the king commanded, and they brought Daniel, and cast him into the den of lions. And the king spake and said unto him, "Thy God whom thou servest continually, he will deliver thee." And a stone was brought, and laid upon the mouth of the den.

Then the king went to his palace, and passed the night fasting: neither were instruments of musick brought before him: and his sleep went from him.

Then the king arose very early in the morning, and went in haste unto the den of lions. And he cried with a lamentable voice unto Daniel: "O Daniel, servant of the living God, is thy God, whom thou servest continually, able to deliver thee from the lions?"

Then said Daniel unto the king, "O king, live for ever. My God hath sent his angel, and hath shut the lions' mouths, that they have not hurt me."

Then was the king exceeding glad for Daniel, and commanded that he be taken up out of the den. So Daniel was taken up, and no manner of hurt was found upon him, because he believed in his God.

Then King Darius wrote unto all people, nations and languages, that dwell in all the earth: "Peace be multiplied unto you. I make a decree, That in every dominion of my kingdom men tremble and fear before the God of Daniel: for he is the living God, and steadfast for ever, and his kingdom that which shall not be destroyed, and his dominion shall be even unto the end. He delivereth and rescueth, and he worketh signs and wonders in heaven and in earth, who hath delivered Daniel from the power of the lions."

❖   DANIEL 6   ❖

INDEX OF PAINTINGS

FRONT COVER
God Creating the Earth (detail)
RAFFAELLO SANZIO, RAPHAEL
(1483-1520)
VATICAN
By the young age of 26, the Italian artist Raphael was already considered to be equal to the great Michelangelo. This painting, among others, was commissioned for a room in the Vatican. God's classic pose, with outstretched arms and a billowing red cloak, is typical of Raphael's style. A lion is placed close to God, befitting its stature as King of the Beasts.

PAGE 9
The Creation of the Animals (detail)
JACOPO ROBUSTI TINTORETTO
(1518-94)
GALLERIA DELL'ACCADEMIA, VENICE
Tintoretto was a Venetian painter with a gift for dramatic story-telling. The way most of the animals are streaming across the painting in the same direction as the brilliantly lit figure of God, suggests the painting may be part of a frieze.

PAGE 10
The Garden of Eden (detail)
JAN VAN KESSEL, THE ELDER
(1626-79)
PRIVATE COLLECTION
A Flemish still-life painter, famous for his detailed miniatures, here van Kessel has painted mouth-watering fruit and beautiful flowers. His use of blue and green suggests calmness and peace. Adam and Eve appear in miniature in the middle distance.

PAGE 13
Adam and Eve in the Garden of Eden (detail)
LUCAS CRANACH, THE ELDER
(1472-1553)
KUNSTHISTORISCHES MUSEUM, VIENNA
Cranach's name derives from his birthplace, Kronach in Germany. In 1505 he became court painter to the Electors of Saxony at Wittenburg. This detailed painting, completed in 1530, shows the whole story of Adam and Eve: in the background, we see God creating Eve out of Adam's side, and Adam eating the forbidden fruit from the Tree of Knowledge. The couple hide from the anger of God in the bushes, only to be chased out of Eden by a fierce angel.

PAGES 5 AND 14
The Animals Entering the Ark (detail)
JACOB SAVERY II
(1593-1627)
PRIVATE COLLECTION
The image teems with animal life, showing off the artist's skill. The dark sky above the little village suggests the onset of the terrible rainstorms which will destroy the land.

PAGE 16
Noah and his Family after the Flood (detail)
FRANCESCO BASSANO
(1549-92)

PRIVATE COLLECTION

Son of Jacopo Bassano, Francesco was a member of the family of Venetian painters working in Bassano. In the far distance we can see Noah praying and lighting a sacrificial fire to thank God. The smoke of the fire links with the radiant light of the sun. The artist has successfully taken us on a journey from dark to light, from a domestic to a heavenly scene.

PAGE 19
The Tower of Babel (detail)
PIETER BRUEGEL, THE ELDER
(c.1515–69)

KUNSTHISTORISCHES MUSEUM, VIENNA

Bruegel was a great Netherlandish artist, strongly influenced by Hieronymous Bosch. This allegory of the Tower of Babel illustrates the folly of building such a gigantic, complex structure against the will of God – it is more like a fortress than a tower. Bruegel shows its immense height in comparison to the tiny size of the people building it.

PAGE 21
Abraham and Isaac (detail)
JOHANN HEINRICH FERDINAND OLIVIER
(1785–1841)

NATIONAL GALLERY, LONDON

Olivier was born in Dessau, Germany. He settled in Vienna in 1811 and became part of a circle of Romantic writers and artists. The stern figure of Abraham is shown carrying a fiery torch, and a knife is hidden in the folds of his blue robe. His face is almost mask-like while Isaac, his son, looks delicate in his pale costume. The artist surrounds the figures with a very detailed landscape based on his studies of the countryside around Salzburg.

PAGE 22
Eliezer and Rebecca at the Well c. 1660 (detail)
NICOLAS POUSSIN
(1594-1665)

FITZWILLIAM MUSEUM, UNIVERSITY OF CAMBRIDGE

Poussin was born in France but settled in Rome after 1624. He led the life of an artist-philosopher, painting and meditating among the Roman ruins and hills. Typical of Poussin's work, this image is perfectly balanced: the shape of the column is echoed by the girl on the far right, carrying a water jug on her head; the kneeling servant in the brightly coloured cloak is mirrored by the kneeling lady.

44

PAGE 24

Joseph's Brothers beg for Help (detail)
PONTORMO
(1494–1557)

THE NATIONAL GALLERY, LONDON

Pontormo, an Italian, was influenced by the German artist
Dürer. A deeply religious man, he led a solitary life: his
studio was accessible only by means of a ladder which he
could pull up after himself. Inscribed on the banner on the
right of the painting are the words, 'ECCE SALVATOR
MUNDI', 'Behold the Saviour of the World', emphasising
the parallel between the lives of Joseph and Christ.

PAGES 29 AND BACK COVER

The Crossing of the Red Sea (detail)
COSIMO ROSSELLI
(1439–1507)

VATICAN, SISTINE CHAPEL

Rosselli was a Florentine painter. He played an important
part in the decoration of the Sistine Chapel under the
direction of Botticelli. The fresco is symbolically divided
into two distinct halves: on one side we see dark threatening
skies and a chaotic scene of the Egyptians attempting to
cross the Sea; on the other, the trees, rocks and Israelites are
bathed in a yellow light, suggesting calmness and peace.

PAGE 31

**Moses with the Tables of the Law
and the Adoration of the Golden Calf**
COSIMO ROSSELLI
(1439–1507)

VATICAN, SISTINE CHAPEL

This fresco was painted between 1481 and 1483. It combines
a number of events in one picture: Moses receiving the Ten
Commandments on Mount Sinai, his journey down the
mountain and his anger at witnessing the Israelites
worshipping the Golden Calf. There is a stark contrast
between the elaborate, rich clothes of the Israelites and the
simplicity of Moses in his unadorned robes.

PAGE 26

The Finding of Moses (detail)
GIOVANNI BATTISTA TIEPOLO
(1696–1770)

NATIONAL GALLERY OF SCOTLAND, EDINBURGH

The Venetian artist Tiepolo was the master of light and
shadow – notice the dark and slightly sinister colours of the
men contrasting with the brilliant highlights of the women's
elegant dresses. Pharaoh's daughter is placed high against a
light sky. The swirling, silvery grey cloak and pale limbs of
the baby, almost falling out of the picture, add drama and
movement to the scene.

PAGE 33

Landscape with Ruth and Boaz
JOSEF ANTON KOCH
(1768–1839)

PRIVATE COLLECTION

The artist was a German landscape painter, influenced by
Poussin. This painting is one of five recorded oils by Koch
on the subject. Ruth is kneeling before Boaz who points to
a group of people reaping and scything in the fields. Our
eye travels in this direction, across the golden fields, giving a
feeling of space which is enhanced by the artist's use of pale
colours in the distance.

PAGE 34
David and Jonathan (detail)
GIOVANNI BATTISTA CIMA DA CONEGLIANO
(*c.*1459/60–*c.*1517/18)
NATIONAL GALLERY, LONDON

One of the trademarks of Cima's paintings is his love of small villages and pleasant landscapes. Here, David is casually carrying the massive hairy head of Goliath, the giant, while Jonathan, King Saul's son, gazes admiringly at him.

PAGE 37
The Judgment of Solomon (detail)
GIORGIONE
(1476/8–1510)
GALLERIA DEGLI UFFIZI, FLORENCE

Most of Giorgione's life is shrouded in mystery. His works are hard to date and he died young from the plague. In this image we see that over half the canvas is taken up by trees, fields and rocks, suggesting the artist's love of nature.

PAGE 39
Belshazzar's Feast (detail)
REMBRANDT
(1606–1669)
THE NATIONAL GALLERY, LONDON

Rembrandt was born in Leiden, Holland, and became the most influential Dutch artist of the 17th century. Here, Rembrandt contrasts the clothes and rich jewels of King Belshazzar with the ghostly hand, emerging from a dark cloud, and writing a message in Hebrew on the wall. The drama is emphasized through the abrupt movement of the King and the terrified figures surrounding him.

PAGE 40
Daniel in the Lions' Den
PETER PAUL RUBENS
(1577–1640)
NATIONAL GALLERY OF ART, WASHINGTON (AILSA MELLON BRUCE FUND)

Rubens was born in Flanders. He spent several years in Italy and was greatly influenced by Titian, Carracci and Caravaggio. He settled in Antwerp in 1608, continuing his career as both painter and diplomat. He cleverly draws us into this dramatic scene via the snarling lion, crouched over a skull and bones in the foreground. Rubens' realistic painting of the lions' fur came from his sketches of lions drawn in the Royal Zoo, Brussels.

PHOTOGRAPHIC ACKNOWLEDGEMENTS

For permission to reproduce the paintings on the following pages and for supplying photographs, the Publishers thank:

BRIDGEMAN ART LIBRARY, LONDON: Front cover, 9, 13, 19, 37

CHRISTIE'S, LONDON/BRIDGEMAN ART LIBRARY, LONDON: 5, 14

FITZWILLIAM MUSEUM, UNIVERSITY OF CAMBRIDGE/BRIDGEMAN ART LIBRARY, LONDON: 22

THE NATIONAL GALLERY, LONDON: 21, 24, 34, 39

© 1996 BOARD OF TRUSTEES, NATIONAL GALLERY OF ART, WASHINGTON: 40

NATIONAL GALLERY OF SCOTLAND, EDINBURGH: 26

SCALA, FLORENCE: 29, 31, back cover

SOTHEBY'S, LONDON: 16, 33

JOHNNY VAN HAEFTEN LTD., LONDON/BRIDGEMAN ART LIBRARY, LONDON: 10